ROGER FITE

MISPLACED COWBOY Writings

Lessons on Faith, Resilience, and God's Unfailing Love

Misplaced Cowboy Writings

© 2025 Roger Fite All Rights Reserved

Performance Publishing Group
McKinney, TX

All Worldwide Rights Reserved.
All rights reserved. No part of this publication may be reproduced, stored in a retrieval system or transmitted, in any form or by any means, electronic, mechanical, recorded, photocopied, or otherwise, without the prior written permission of the copyright owner, except by a reviewer who may quote brief passages in a review.

Cover Artwork
"Spring Range" by Tim Cox
Courtesy of Tim Cox Western Paintings & Fine Art
www.timcox.com

ISBN:
Hardcover: 978-1-961781-80-1
Softcover: 978-1-961781-88-7

TESTIMONIALS FOR MISPLACED COWBOY WRITINGS

Roger Fite has given us words of wisdom, compassion, challenge, and truth. Though he wears boots and says he is a "Misplaced Cowboy", his heart is missionary and his feet are shod with the Gospel of Peace!

-Tony Gray,
Pioneer Missions Global

In Roger Fite's writing are the same transparency and rawness that have characterized the greatest verse and prose for centuries. Coupled with his insightful interpretation of universal themes and his ability to always find God's beauty and loving work in every corner of life, this work is sure to help readers dealing with certain parts of the human experience find deeper meaning in both trials and triumphs. It is a book that I will revisit often.

-Gentry Sutton, D.Ed.Min.
President, Warner University

"I grew up loving cowboys and always admired their simple way of explaining life. **Misplaced Cowboy Writings** is a book that brings nostalgia but in a way that challenges me to think outside of yesteryear. Roger Fite has a way of telling his stories that brings back memories but makes you realize the lessons he learned have a broad application. It is a helpful book you will enjoy and put to good use."

-Mike Means
Oklahoma Home Builders Association

Roger Fite is a great storyteller. His wisdom, emotion, and transparency will encourage everyone in their faith journey.

-Robin Marsh
KWTV Anchor

TABLE OF CONTENTS

Chapter 1   HOPE 1
                 Spiritual Hope 3
                 The Hope of Knowing 4
                 The Seed 5
                 The Vessel of Honor 9
                 When Hope is Strategic 11

Chapter 2   BE STILL and KNOW 13
                 A Touch of Pentecost 15
                 Be still and know. 18
                 El Elyon 19
                 The Hummingbird 21
                 What if? 23
                 Praise. 26

Chapter 3   LOVE 27
                 The Anvil 29
                 I Choose Love 30
                 Beautiful Fabric 31
                 The Auditorium of Love. 32
                 The Circle 33
                 Your Child on a Cross? 34

Chapter 4	LOSS 37	
	Sunrise 39	
	The Eulogy 40	
	The Gift 45	
Chapter 5	LOVE AGAIN 49	
	The Journey 51	
	Seasonal Flowers 53	
	The Orcas 55	
	The Canyons of Our Hearts 57	
Chapter 6	LIFE 59	
	Live like it's Heaven 60	
	Pursue Your Dreams 61	
	The Cover 63	
	The Wounded Goose 65	
	Words of Life 67	
	The Image of God 68	

FOREWORD

It was my joy to be a pastor for over forty-five years. During those many years, I met many people who had a special place in serving the Lord. Roger Fite was one of those people. You are about to read a wonderful book concerning Roger's life. As you read, you will find yourself and many of your life situations. You will also find answers and encouragement from these words. Roger has called himself "a misplaced cowboy." It is true, as he is a cowboy who has lived much of his life in a large city. But he is certainly not misplaced. He added much to my life, and I'm sure he will add much to your life, as well. God placed him exactly where he needed to be for me. I'm sure you will feel the same as you read his words.

Ted Kersh D. Min.
Bible Teacher
Ted Kersh Ministries

Chapter 1

HOPE

Spiritual Hope

There are spiritual things to do and there are earthly things to do.

There is a spiritual love and a physical love.

There is earthly hope and there is spiritual hope.

All these are necessary for peace, contentment, and happiness in this life.

But of all these, give me spiritual hope in the Living God of the Universe.

He is forever.

The Hope of Knowing

There is a hope that goes beyond believing.

It is a hope of knowing.

It is a hope of knowing that life is more than science.

It is knowing there is a Creator.

It is knowing and trusting so completely in the Almighty, Omnipresent, Omnipotent God, that doubts have no place.

It is knowing there is a place of existence with such unimaginable beauty, that words of language cannot describe.

It is a hope that stretches across the horizon into forever. All the images of beauty in our minds of majestic mountains, of serene meadows, of creatures we love are only the beginnings of that hope.

Some call it heaven. Some call it the New Earth.

Our visions of life and love are shallow in comparison to the reality of that hope.

Yes, it's that and more.

It is the home of God Almighty.

It is a hope of now and forever.

It is a hope of knowing.

The Seed

The countryside looked like Oklahoma. It was flat land fading into rolling hills. Extensive wheat farming and cattle were the main economic industries in the area. The soil was some of the richest in the world.

I had been to Brazil several times previously but never this far south. We were assisting a local church congregation with the construction of a chapel. The farming community was only a few miles from the Argentine border.

It was primarily a German immigrant settlement and the German language was spoken as often as Portuguese. It was ethnically different than all the previous missions I had led or assisted on. The team I had brought to this area of the world was welcomed warmly by the locals and invited into their homes.

As I had done in other areas of South America, I took every opportunity to canvas the area and share about our mission. Most importantly, I would share the gospel as often as possible.

On this day, I had been invited into a home where three middle age women were enjoying their afternoon tea. My translator was the daughter of a pastor from another town in that southern state. She was of German descent and was fluent in Portuguese, German, and English. She was an invaluable asset God had provided for the project.

The women were very open and listened intently to every word spoken. After some interesting social conversation, I asked if I could share the gospel with them for a few minutes. They asked me to continue.

I read the scriptures and spoke of how our Heavenly Father had sent his Son to pay the price for our sins. I told of God's love for all people and how it was His will that no one should perish. I spoke of the sin in our lives that keeps us from having a relationship with Holy God. I explained that there is no other way to Heaven except through Jesus and that no one can save themselves by good works alone. This seemed to be a revelation to many in the area who had been taught that their salvation was based upon the life they lived.

Two of the women eagerly accepted my teaching of the gospel that day. They looked forward to the opportunity to attend the local church where the construction team was building the chapel.

The third woman graciously denied the opportunity afforded her. She indicated that she did not need God as her life was just fine the way it was. I thanked her for the invitation to share and continued on. We had planted the seed and the growth was up to God.

1 Corinthians 3:7 Neither the one who plants nor the one who waters is anything, but **God who causes the growth**.

Almost three years later, I received a letter from the translator. She was very happy to report on the progress at the mission church our team had helped to establish. The words seemed to jump off the page as I read her excitement concerning the woman who had indicated she did not need God. The translator wrote of how she had visited the church recently and the woman was there. She explained that the woman had experienced difficult times and had fallen into deep depression. The woman had approached her and spoken with great emotion of how she could not forget the words spoken to her three years earlier. She remembered how I had told of God's great love and how Jesus wanted to be her best friend. She remembered my words that Jesus would always be with her and would never leave her.

The woman had turned her heart to Almighty God and never looked back. She had taken all her family to church, and they, too, had given their hearts to Jesus. They are now active members of the local congregation.

Plant the seed whenever you can.
God will cause the growth.

The Vessel of Honor

It is a small shaving mug displaying no particular brilliance or notable markings. Its color is a natural sandy brown emulating the clay from which it was formed. It is a decagon shape with a lead-poured bottom for stability. It has a chip on the edge of the flared top. It has not cracked or broken.

The mug belonged to my ancestor, seven generations past. That ancestor's name is carved on the bottom of the mug. It was crafted by a potter over two hundred fifty years ago.

I cherish the vessel, and it is displayed on a shelf in my home. Its history is proudly narrated to all. To me, it is worth more than fine gold. It is a vessel of honor.

Have you ever felt that your life has little value?

Are you the father who toils long hours only to achieve a meager existence for your family?

Are you the mother who has lost her husband and struggles daily? Your loneliness is deafening. The only thing that seems to keep you going are the eyes of the small children peering over the edge of the bed as you force yourself to rise after each long night.

Are you the young person who always seems to be at the back of the line of opportunity?

Do you feel like the small brown mug of little value? God knows your existence. He knows your struggles. Life has been hard, but you have been faithful. Your Heavenly Father knows all these things. Your faithfulness will be rewarded.

One day, you will be displayed with honor by the Potter.

You are a special treasure to God.

You are a vessel of honor.

When Hope is Strategic

Hope is strategic?

How can that be?

Is it good to have Hope in all things we endeavor to do? Absolutely! But it is not a strategy. It is not a plan.

We plan our future. We study and learn in the vocation of our choice. We plan and hope for the best.

The athlete works and conditions for a winning outcome. He hopes to raise his arms in the winner's circle. But he plans the path to achieve that goal.

The gifted musician hopes to be the best in his field. He hopes for that goal. But his path to achieve it is marked by much work and dedication. This is his strategy.

We encounter various difficulties. We hope to overcome and conquer these trials. But we plan our path to climb the hills and mountains before us.

But hope in the living God of the universe is strategic. When we trust and hope in the Creator, the Redeemer, the Sovereign, the God of the universe... it is strategy.

It is everything.

Chapter 2

BE STILL and KNOW

SOUTH AMERICA
BOLIVIA
La Paz
Potosi
Tarija
PARAGUAY
Asunción
Foz do Iguacu
Iguazu Falls
Curitiba
Sao Paulo
Campinas
Maringa
Posadas
Formosa
Resistencia
Corrientes
Rio Parana
Porto Alegre
Santa Maria
Pelotas
Rio Grande
Salto
Melo
URUGUAY
Montevideo
Buenos Aires
La Plata
Rosario
Sante Fe
Cordoba
Laguna Mar Chiquita
La Rioja
Tucuman
Salta
San Salvador
San Juan
Mendoza
San Luis
Santiago
ARGENTINA
Santa Rosa
ANDES MOUNTAINS
CHILE
Tocopilla
Antofagasta
Taltal
Copiapo
Huasco
La Serena
Vina del Mar
Valparaiso
San Antonio
Iquique
Arica
CHILE
BASIN

A Touch of Pentecost

Acts 2:1-4 When the day of Pentecost had come, they were all together in one place. ² And suddenly there came from heaven a noise like a violent rushing wind, and it filled the whole house where they were sitting. ³And there appeared to them tongues as a fire distributing themselves and they rested on each one of them. ⁴And they were all filled with the Holy Spirit and began to speak with other languages.

Acts 2:7-8 They were amazed and astonished, saying "How is it that we each hear them in our own language to which we were born?"

Acts 2:14-40 Peter, taking his stand, raised his voice and declared how Jesus had died for all.

Acts 2:41 Those who had received his word were baptized; and that day there were added about 3000 souls.

I had assisted with the construction of two previous chapels. I had also organized and led two other chapel construction projects in Brazil.

I am a custom home builder by occupation in Oklahoma. I had teamed with a missionary in Brazil that was from South Carolina. Accordingly, the mission volunteers in Brazil were from both states.

We had arrived on Saturday, and much preparation for the project had been accomplished. Although I am a builder by trade, my great love is to share my faith in Jesus Christ.

It was late Monday morning, and there had been little time to go through the community and meet the local residents. All seemed to be flowing well with the construction aspect of the mission. I informed our team that I was going to go through the neighborhood to meet and share with some of the local Brazilians. I took an interpreter and a young local Brazilian who knew the area.

I had developed a tradition of praying for God's hand to be upon us as we went and for His Spirit to go in front of us to prepare the way. I would usually pray and allow the interpreter to pray in the local language (Portuguese in this case) so all would understand the prayer. However, as it was late morning and things had been somewhat rushed, I did not take the time for the interpreter to translate the prayer.

It was a relatively short prayer. As I started praying, the young Brazilian lady prayed, also. It was different but somehow seemed special.

As we proceeded down the street, I was leading with the interpreter and young lady behind me. I could hear them talking in Portuguese but had no idea what the conversation was. After a short time, they stopped and were continuing their discussion. I turned and asked, "Is there a problem?"

The interpreter seemed very confused. He had assumed the young Brazilian knew English. The interpreter was astonished to hear that she knew absolutely no English.

I asked, "What is astonishing about that?"

I was speechless and dumbstruck when the interpreter said, "She repeated your prayer almost word for word as you were praying!"

After gathering our emotions, it was obvious we felt a sense of God's presence about us.

As we topped a hill, we overlooked the main street of the community. As we descended, one of the first structures was a local bar and pool hall. It was filled with several young men, enjoying their pool, snooker, and beer.

I indicated to the interpreter and young guide that I'd like to stop and share about the church construction with the occupants.

"Oh no, Christians are not allowed in bars," she said.

Trying to dispel her fears, I said, "Let's just stop and say hello."

We were met with a wary reception. As I began to introduce myself and show interest in their game, it was obvious there was a leader among the group. As they were young men of an athletic appearance, I asked if they were involved with any sports. As Brazilians take great pride in their soccer abilities, this opened the door for extended conversation. I had two sons in Oklahoma who were involved in American football and basketball.

After fielding many questions from them about sports in the U.S., I asked the group if I could share for a few moments about something very important. This caused a hushed tone among the group. After a few seconds, the leader looked around and instructed the other young men to lay their pool cues on the snooker table. After they gathered around the table, I shared how God had sent his Son to redeem them. They listened intently as I told how Jesus died their death on a cross to give them life.

After I finished, the leader of that group in the bar that day, along with eight other young men, accepted Jesus as Lord and Savior.

I did not know Portuguese. She did not know English.

A touch of Pentecost in Brazil.

Be still and know.

Be still! What does that mean?

No motion? No sound? Yes, that and more.

Being still and knowing involves a trust that is unnatural. It is faith in God to affect the best outcome for our lives.

It may be cloudy, snowy, or rainy. There may be storm clouds all around. But our Lord and God is still there, laying the groundwork of amazing things for those who love Him.

And yes, being still means waiting on Him. It is so hard to wait. We must realize that waiting is part of love. It is being silent with no motion, trusting Him.

It means having unwavering faith in Jehovah. And when the storm clouds clear, our Creator smiles as we walk through the doors He opens for us.

We want to help Him. We want to push the doors open. But God, who loves us as his special treasure, doesn't want us pushing closed doors. He wants us to wait on Him as He gently opens them and reveals the wonderful blessings He has for us.

Be still and know.

Psalm 46:10 Be still, and know that I am God; I will be exalted among the nations, I will be exalted in the earth.

El Elyon

Do you know, with certainty, that nothing occurs in your daily world that does not fall under God's control?

Do you know that nothing in the universe can touch your life except by His permission and filtered through His fingers of love?

He is Elohim, the Creator.

He is El Elyon, the sovereign most high God.

The Hummingbird

God does not perform miracles today.

There are no more miracles like the parting of the Red Sea. No turning the water into wine as Jesus did at the wedding feast.

I have heard these proclamations all too often.

Oh, but God does perform miracles today! If we open the eyes of our hearts and minds, we will see God's miracles every day and in every place.

Look at all creation. Look at the vastness of the universe and the galaxies.

Observe the earth and its environs and all it contains. Gaze upon its surface. Witness beautiful mountains, the vastness of the oceans and all they hold, and large, powerful animals. All miracles of God's creation.

Life itself is a phenomenon beyond our understanding. All creatures, great and small, are miracles indeed.

Some things elicit amazement and catch our attention more readily than others.

But what about the smallest and most intricate workings of physics? How did such a chain of reactions, events, and creations happen? The chance happenings of these cannot be calculated.

Consider the smallest bird of the sky, the hummingbird.

They are from two to nine inches long. They beat their wings up to eighty times per second. The Rufus hummingbird migrates almost 4000 miles (one of the longest migrations of all animals). They weigh from .02 to .85 ounces. When food is scarce, they hibernate at night to conserve their tiny body mass.

Have you ever had a hummingbird hover two feet from your face to check you out?

Have you ever picked up a hummingbird caught in a spiderweb to aid its release? Have you ever held the bird in your hand as you clean the webbing from its tiny wings? Have you then released the bird into the wild to see the tiny creature fly away, and then gasped with amazement as the bird returned to alight once again on your arm to say thank you for your kindness?

Yes, there are miracles today.

The greatest of these is the love of the Creator for His creation. The creation He made in His image. A love so vast and so indescribable that he gave a savior to redeem us.

God sent his spirit in the form of a dove to descend upon Jesus.

He made the hummingbird.

Be still and know.

What if?

It was a hot July day in Brazil. Although South American seasons are reversed to those in the Northern Hemisphere, winters there are still very hot. The equatorial climate is challenging. I was on a mission project assisting my pastor friend. We each had an interpreter as we split up to canvas different areas of the community.

It had been a long day of door-to-door sharing about the ongoing revival being held in their community. As opportunity arose, I would share my faith in Jesus. Some would embrace and accept my words, some would not.

It had been a very successful day, and it was time to return to our designated meeting location.

As we were returning, a certain home caught my attention. It was a nice but modest home with no particular features that distinguished it from others. I asked my Brazilian guide "Who lives there?"

The guide indicated that the residents were of a different faith and would not want them to stop. "Besides," she said, "we are late to return."

"I believe we should stop and meet them," I said. We knocked on the door and were met by a young lady and her mother. We were invited in to visit.

I shared the purpose of our travel to their community. The mother and daughter listened with great focus and enthusiasm. I shared how Jesus paid such a great price for us so we might have eternal life. As I talked about the love of God the Father and His plan to redeem us, the eyes of the daughter glistened as she could barely hold back from interrupting.

I asked, "Did you understand what I shared?"

The daughter replied with teary eyes, "Oh yes, I understand." She continued, "About six months prior, someone at my school gave me a New Testament. I knew I needed God, but I didn't know what to do. I somehow knew someone would come to show me, and I've been waiting for you!"

I've been waiting for you. Those words, spoken that day, will forever be etched on my heart and mind.

What if I had chosen not to go on the mission project with my friend?

What if I had not listened as God tugged at my heart to stop at the house of the young lady who was waiting for me?

What if? What if?

What if you had not taken those homemade cookies to your neighbor who so needed to see an act of kindness? You had no idea her despair had brought her so low.

What if you had not asked your friend to lunch? You had no idea he so needed to hear a caring heart.

God wants to use you and bless you as you honor him with your kindness.

The closer we walk with our creator, the more we hear that still small voice.

What if?

SOUTH AMERICA
BOLIVIA
La Paz
Sucre
Potosi
Santa Cruz
Villa Martin
Tarija
Arica
Iquique
Tocopilla
Antofagasta
Taltal
CHILE
Copiapo
Huasco
La Serena
Vina del Mar
Valparaiso
San Antonio
Santiago
Rancagua
ANDES MOUNTAINS
San Salvador
Salta
Tucuman
La Rioja
Laguna Mar Chiquita
Cordoba
Sante Fe
Rosario
San Juan
Mendoza
San Luis
Buenos Aires
La Plata
ARGENTINA
Santa Rosa
Mar del Plata
PARAGUAY
Asuncion
Formosa
Resistencia
Corrientes
Posadas
Rio Parana
Foz do Iguacu
Iguazu Falls
Campo Grande
Pedro Juan Caballero
Maringa
Campinas
Sao Paulo
Curitiba
Porto Alegre
Santa Maria
Pelotas
Rio Grande
Salto
URUGUAY
Montevideo

Praise.

Praise.

It is the verbal glorification of Almighty God.

Music? All kinds of music?

Absolutely.

God loves our praise.

God wants our praise.

We will eternally praise Him in heaven and beyond.

What type of music does He cherish the most?

He accepts all types of music if they are offered to Him with the love and adoration He deserves.

Does He have favorites? Probably.

His favorite praise is not composed of wonderful notes sung by talented voices or gifted sounds of instruments.

Yes, He loves that praise.

But the greatest praise is the beautiful music through the voice of our lives as we give all to Him.

God smiles and dances with joy as He listens to the greatest praise offered to Him.

Let us sing forever.

Chapter 3
LOVE

The Anvil

God's anvil is very hard. The pain of his molding can seem unbearable at times. The heat of his forge is excruciating. But the Master knows of the treasure He is creating. A vessel created for love.

I have loved and been loved. I have known love that will never die.

I love again with a passion I thought was lost in time and space of this life.

We are vessels created for love. We were forged by Love Himself. God is love.

I love.

I Choose Love

Love is an amazing God-given feeling.

It can reach unbelievable heights.

Love can propel us to unfathomable emotions.

But love can cause indescribable pain and agony of our souls.

Someone unaware of the anguish of love may ask, "Was it worth it to suffer such great loss?"

I would answer, "If I lived another 1000 years or more, I would choose love into eternity."

Beautiful Fabric

As we live the lives God has ordained for us, we encounter various trials and distresses.

As we walk the path he has chosen for us, we will experience joy and celebrations.

All will become memories in the gallery of our minds.

The anvil and the feast will both be thoughts of art. We will forever observe them with great thankfulness.

We will reflect and know the Sovereign Creator wove each into a beautiful fabric pleasing to Him

The Auditorium of Love.

Love is a symphony composed by God himself. It is a performance like no other.

Love's instruments are various and sometimes anonymous. They're made of kindness, sacrifice, dedication, and compassion. There are no instruments of selfishness and betrayal. The harmonious music created is action and service. It is a symphony of love.

The auditorium has assigned seating. There's a seat for all in the auditorium. Not all will attend. It is a choice.

I want to be there to hear and relish every note. As I take my assigned seat at the concert, I look at who is seated next to me. I see you.

The symphony is like no other.

Its composer is God.

The Circle

He drew a circle around his life that shut her out, but love would not let him win.

She drew a larger circle that took him in.

Note: This was sent to me as a young man by my mother, Mary Jo Fite, during a difficult time in my life.

Your Child on a Cross?

I am not a preacher, pastor, evangelist, or any other seminary-trained man of God. I am just an ordinary working man. But God has touched my heart to be involved with volunteer missions.

On this day, I was leading a team to construct a church building in Brazil. I had been to South America a few times before. However, this was my first project to lead a team without a pastor. The celebratory worship in the newly constructed chapel was on Friday night, at the end of the project. The local pastor asked me to bring the message.

I did not feel qualified. Who would want to hear a misplaced cowboy from Oklahoma stumble over his words in the pulpit? I did not have a flowing three-point sermon to share with the congregation.

As I stepped upon the small stage, constructed that week, and took my place behind the wooden pulpit our team had built, I could feel my hands tremble. *What am I doing here*, I thought. *All I can do is thank them for allowing me and the volunteer mission team to be a part of their vision for God's kingdom.*

God took over. I shared the team's appreciation, as each volunteer had grown to love the local congregation. I expressed my sincere desire for God's hand to be upon their community, and that God would use them as a shining light that would permeate throughout that area of the world.

As I paused and gazed into the eyes of the congregation, I knew not all at the celebration were believers. I spoke of how Holy

God created us all and loves us as His special creation. I spoke of the sin in our lives that separates us from God the Father. I shared that a righteous and Holy God hates sin and cannot leave it unpunished. I explained in detail how the Father gave his own Son as a sacrifice for all of humanity.

As I finished describing the death of Jesus on the cross, of the pain and suffering the Son had endured, I stopped and looked around at the audience. As I had gotten to know the local congregation, I then asked one of the young women, "Aline, could you give your son to die on a cross for anyone?"

She tearfully hung her head and, with a broken voice, said, "No, I could not."

I then asked the congregation, "Could anyone here nail your child to a cross to suffer and die for another?" I continued, "I can't comprehend that kind of love. But that's the love God has for you."

Could you nail your child to a wooden cross?

Chapter 4

LOSS

Sunrise

For seven days, the skies had been overcast with ominous clouds and intermittent rain. For seven days, her eyes were closed. The only response I received from her was a gentle nod when I asked, "Do you know how much I love you?"

The skies were dark and the nights were long during this week of suffering.

On Friday morning, May 27, 2022, at 6:22 a.m., as I held her hand, stroked her hair, felt that last pulse, and heard that last gasp of breath, a wonderful sunrise from on high visited the room. My Michelle suffered no more. It was a stunningly beautiful morning.

She was in Paradise.

Sunrise on May 27, 2022, was exactly at 6:22 a.m.

Luke 1:78 Because of the tender mercy of our God, the **Sunrise from on high will visit us**.

The Eulogy

She was the love of my life. Our marriage had experienced forty-four years of love, joy, and heartache. It was a marriage made in heaven. It was not a perfect union, but it was God-centered.

She was not yet sixty-six years old when God took her home. She had finally succumbed to a rare liver disease. I was heartbroken and devastated. But I knew the pain and suffering she had experienced for twelve years. I was relieved that she was no longer suffering and was in the arms of her Lord and Savior whom she loved so much. I loved her beyond description, but in the ensuing days, I would come to realize the awesome depth of the love we had known.

On this day, one week after her passing, her memorial service was held. It was still in the latter days of the COVID-19 pandemic, and I was not sure how many would venture out to attend her funeral. She had been adamant that any service held in her wake would not be about her but about our awesome God and His sovereign hand upon our lives.

I attempted to plan her funeral service according to her request. However, I did something out of the ordinary that I never spoke of with her. I gave her eulogy myself. I felt that no one else could share her wonderful life with the passion and praise she deserved.

I was amazed at the number of people who traveled to her funeral from across the country. It was surely a testament to the life and example she had been to so many.

I had spoken many times in a public forum. Normally, I only take talking points with me to the podium. Today, I wrote out what I wanted everyone to hear as I feared I might be unable to finish. If this happened, one of my sons would be able to finish the eulogy.

I walked to the podium, shook the hands of the pastors officiating, then turned to face the audience and begin. I took a long moment to gaze at the audience and memorize those who had come to honor the life of one so very well lived.

I began.

She was beautiful.

She was born in Oklahoma and later moved to New Mexico. She grew up on the grounds of the Glorietta Baptist Retreat and Conference Center where her father was the financial manager. She attended high school in Santa Fe, New Mexico. She attended college at Central State University in Oklahoma after transferring from the University of New Mexico. This is where our world and life together began.

She liked to tell of how we met. I hope I can relay this story to you today with the same excitement and gleam she had in her eyes as she told others. As she was attending the university, she had a part-time job at a local bank. She was a drive-through bank teller, and I had an account at the bank. I was working in the area and also had a small farm and ranch operation some distance away.

Once, as I was going through the drive-through lane, I looked up and saw the most beautiful eyes and face. My initial thought was, *What a gorgeous wife someone has*. I would continue to go through that lane several times. She got a bit perturbed at my numerous requests for a countercheck. She would have to go inside and look up my account number. She eventually posted my number on the wall for easier reference. Despite my antics to get her attention, I devised one last plan to get noticed. One afternoon, I had purchased a large bull from a ranch north of the area where she worked. I had loaded the bull in an open-top stock trailer, and I took the animal through the drive-through lane. I GOT HER ATTENTION! You can imagine the reaction when the critter, weighing almost a ton, looked over the top of the trailer.

Fortunately, the rest is history, as she was not married. God had saved her for me.

A few months after we started dating, we went to a cafeteria for lunch. We were in the serving line and a prominent Oklahoma sportscaster was in front of us. I have no idea why I picked that spot, but all at once, I asked her to marry me. She looked at me, and before she could answer, I made her one of the most ridiculous promises ever. I said, "If you marry me, I promise to build you a new home and never go bald!" I think my impromptu proposal must've been great entertainment for the sportscaster and others who were listening. As God would have it, I started a custom home construction business some years later and built her more than one. The second promise was much harder to keep. Be careful what you promise someone!

We were married in Santa Fe, New Mexico. That union lasted almost forty-four years. We had a wonderful marriage. Like all marriages, we had our differences, but we grew together spiritually and that bond held us together. **We lived a love story.**

We lost three babies in midterm pregnancy. We almost gave up trying for children but decided to try once more. God, in his infinite mercy and love, gave us two great sons after that. These two sons gave us five beautiful grandchildren. She loved her family so very much. In the last few weeks of her life here on earth, she told me repeatedly that she wasn't afraid to die but wasn't ready to leave her family.

She loved the Lord Jesus. She was a passionate woman. She was passionate about whatever she endeavored to do. She was more passionate about her God than anything else in her life. She loved to study God's word. She led and taught many Bible studies for decades. It was obvious the impact she had on many women she taught and counseled. She was very transparent concerning her relationship with God. She taught with boldness, but with a dry humor so many enjoyed. She kept that wit and humor to the end.

She was very creative and talented with her hands. She was a good seamstress who made quilts, greeting cards, and many other crafts. She did nothing halfway. She was either all in or not at all. She was a wonderful cook, homemaker, and hostess.

She was a great encouragement and prayer warrior for my mission ministry. She could not go overseas with me because of her long-running illness, but she always stood by me.

She was an extremely talented musician who sang at various venues and was encouraged to record but refused. In her high school years, she was a multistate champion vocalist.

She was a great lady. She was a graceful woman who loved to help others.

She struggled long with the disease that wracked her body, but she died as she lived. With class and dignity.

In closing, I say to you, "Don't weep for her. Cry for me and the void in my heart if you want. Weep for my family as we loved her so very much. But don't weep for her. She is home."

She was the love of my life. She was my soulmate. I will miss her dearly.

She was beautiful.

Proverbs 31:10 An excellent wife who can find?

Proverbs 31:25 Strength and dignity are her clothing, and she smiles at the future.

Proverbs 31:30 A woman who fears the Lord, she will be praised.

Do you have a Godly wife? Love her, hold her, and cherish her all the days of your fleeting life. **Her worth is more than all the treasures this world can ever give.**

July 6, 1956 -May 27, 2022
Michelle Fite at 50 years of age.

The Gift

She had conquered a bout with cancer once before. When the doctor told her that the cancer had returned, she was devastated.

She was only forty-three years old, and her life had been filled with countless struggles and disappointments.

Her parents had divorced when she was five years old and that trauma had a lasting effect on her. It had disrupted the stability she had known in her young life, and she had never regained that comfort and consistency.

She was a beautiful girl with athletic ability envied by many. Her smile and personality were captivating with the sweetness she portrayed.

But inside, she fought the demons of loneliness and depression. She had listened to the lies of the drug culture and had fallen into a deep pit of dependency.

Her life was a struggle. Failed marriages, economic struggles, and the lonely road of a single mother had left her as a vulnerable prey to those who would take advantage of her plight.

The pit was deep. But God and his infinite mercy reached down and pulled her out. She accepted God's great gift of Jesus's sacrifice for her. She understood the depth of God's love for her. She finally grasped how great the price that was paid as the penalty for our failings. Her eyes were opened to see how God the Father sent His son Jesus to die in our place. A terrible death by torture on a cross. She knew she could now endure whatever trials were in her path. The gleam in her eyes as she acknowledged Him with a thankful heart was inspiring. She anticipated the future with joy.

1 John 10:27-30 My sheep hear my voice, and I know them, and they follow Me; ²⁸and I give eternal life to them, and they will never perish; and no one will snatch them out of My hand. ²⁹ My Father, who has given them to Me, is greater than all; and no one is able to snatch them out of the Father's hand. ³⁰ I and the Father are one.

Then, in her forty-third year, those words, "The cancer has returned," were crushing. She called me, as I lived in another city, and I immediately made plans to come to her aid.

But the panic and devastation were only temporary. God was still holding her hand. She called me again after a short time and said, "Don't worry, Dad. Jesus will see me through. I will be okay."

1 Corinthians 10:13 No temptation has overtaken you, but such as is common to man; and God is faithful, who will not allow you to be tempted beyond what you are able, but with the temptation will provide the way of escape also, that you may be able to endure it.

Thirty days later, on July 1, 2014, she was gone. God took her home. His love did not leave her with a trial she could not endure. No longer would she suffer.

The auto accident that took her life was a sovereign act of a loving Heavenly Father.

She will never again be lonely or depressed. She is home.

It was a gift.

What struggles do you have today that seem overpowering and unconquerable?

Our merciful and loving God is always reaching down with His hand to help you. All you must do is take His hand, and He will never let you go. He will give you indescribable joy to endure whatever you face, and in His time, He will take us home.

The gift of God.

The gift.

July 24, 1969 - July 1, 2013
Sherry Jo Fite

Chapter 5

LOVE AGAIN

The Journey

A man was on a journey with a trusted companion and helper. The King of all creation had sent for them to come and live in His personal Kingdom. It was a very long journey and it required working together and helping each other along the way. The King wanted them to experience their travels and enjoy what He had created.

However, after many days, the King summoned the helper to go with His angels as He had need for the companion immediately at His house. This left the man all alone to carry the load. It was very hard as he now realized how much his companion had carried. She was so much stronger than he had ever known before. The man now knew that those many times he had stumbled and his strength had left him that she had carried his burdens as well as her own.

However, the man knew he must go on. He knew he must somehow find the strength to complete the journey. He knew of the great rewards awaiting. He knew the King would welcome him with open arms. He knew his companion was there. It was very hard.

The man had not gotten far when he met another traveler who had also lost her helper and companion. Her destination was the same as his. *This woman must be very strong*, he thought, as she had traveled with her burden and load much longer than him. Her heartache and loss must have been much like his. They met and had much in common and enjoyed each other's company.

The man decided to go on alone. He had not gone far when the King (always watching over and taking care of His people) sent word to the man to travel with the woman. The King, in His infinite wisdom, knew they needed each other. The man realized that the King had made them both stronger because of the loss of their companions. Together, they now could travel on their journey once again, enjoying life and the King's creation.

Seasonal Flowers

God gave me a flower. Oh, what a beautiful creation it was. It was a choice flower of beauty and fragrance. It was wonderfully crafted by the Creator. Its season was long, but not so long as some. Its time was cut short by an ugly blight.

The season for that flower has passed. It leaves behind memories on the walls of my mind. It leaves behind its likeness, reflected in the seed of its existence.

Thank you, Lord, for eternal images of beauty.

A new season is here. Our amazing God has given another flower. It is different but also beautiful. It, too, is wonderfully crafted by the Creator. It is a fall flower. It is unexpected.

Thank you, God, for this season and this beautiful creation. Thank you for its wonderful aroma that fills my space.

Thank you, Lord.

The Orcas

My Michelle has been gone almost three years now. She was a marvelous and wonderful gift. I will love and miss her until I draw my last breath.

Lynn's Jay left several years ago. The love she has for him is still very alive.

Our sovereign God knows and understands. Jay and Michelle are with Him now. How much they see and know of us that remain we can only imagine. I believe they may be more present with us than we know.

God has given another gift to Lynn and me. A wonderful love for each other. He has chosen for us to unite. The signs and clues of our union being orchestrated and ordained by Him are overwhelming.

I had a dream. Lynn and I were on a ship. She is a good swimmer, I am not. She fell overboard into turbulent waters. I knew I could not save her, but I could try to get her a life preserver. I grabbed one and went into the water. I could not reach her, but I was able to toss the life preserver to her.

I was ready to go home. Our God had other plans. An orca came under me and placed me on its back. It took me safely to shore. It was a female orca.

As Lynn was still struggling, a male orca did the same with her. In the dream, we knew the spirits of Jay and Michelle had entered the orcas to save us from the depths and despair of the turbulent sea. They were placing us on dry land for life together.

Much later, after the dream, Lynn and I were on a ship together off the Alaskan coast. I was alone on the balcony, admiring what our creator had fashioned. I saw the large black fin of an orca, not far from the ship. It submerged and reappeared closer to me. This time, there were two orcas. They were facing me and kept facing me until the ship had passed. To my knowledge, no one else saw the orcas.

Signs and wonders of our gracious and loving God.

The Canyons of Our Hearts

The part of her that I could see and touch was gone. But the most important part of her is still there. She will always be there.

A generation earlier, another suffered great loss. The part she could see and touch was gone. But the most important part of him was still there. He will always be there.

We felt the pain, but God was there. The canyon of her heart was vast. The hole in my heart was deep. On the anvil of time, a Sovereign God placed us together. Our hearts were knit as one.

My Loss and her Loss applaud in heaven at the miracle of a Heavenly Father.

Chapter 6

LIFE

Live like it's Heaven

Work like you don't need the money.

Love like you've never been hurt.

Dance like nobody's watching.

Sing like nobody's listening.

Live like it's Heaven on earth.

Note: Inspired by an old proverb, attributed to different sources over time.

Pursue Your Dreams

Pursue your dreams. Never let time shatter them. Hold them close. Protect them.

If we attain them, it is a gift from God. It's not the quarry, but the chase. It's not the trophy, but the race.

If we remember this, we will win a trophy not made by human hands.

The Cover

Have you ever chosen a book to read based on the cover?

Maybe you chose the book based solely upon the title. Maybe you chose the book based upon the title and the author, which is usually good selection criteria. Many times, surface criteria cause us to read and become acquainted with the narrative inside.

I love history. I love sports. I love art. And being the misplaced cowboy I am, I love most things Western. However, far more beloved than all the aforementioned categories, I love our wonderful, amazing God. As a result, most of the books on the shelves of my home are Christian-related.

The books I tend to read first are the ones with intriguing titles on the cover. If you wrote a book of your life, what would the title be? Far more importantly, would the contents of that book be true to the cover?

Many times in my life, what I portray is not what I want the cover of my book to reflect. When I lose sight of the truth that my life should always reflect our Lord Jesus, I fail miserably.

Am I an inspiration to others? Does my faith have feet? Do I have passion for Godly things above all else?

Do you proclaim a life given wholly and completely to Christ?

What does the title of your life book say?

Would the contents match the cover?

The Wounded Goose

My home reflects a southern style known as a Mississippi Planters Cottage. As such, it has a large front porch that overlooks a small lake. The lake is part of a watershed that attracts much waterfowl.

I enjoy my early morning coffee on the front porch, observing the wildlife that frequents the area. Many geese migrate to the location and some remain the entire summer.

I had noticed a lone goose foraging in my front yard. This goose was different. The bird had a broken and twisted leg. It was extremely handicapped, and its efforts to walk were heartbreaking.

I observed the goose several times over the next few weeks and admired its gallant effort to survive. I concluded that the animal's remaining days were probably few as such a physical handicap left him very vulnerable to predators.

Autumn leaves were now falling, and it had been months since I had observed the handicapped goose in the area. As I was leaving for an early morning appointment, I drove slowly down the long driveway of my home. I stopped to observe a flock of geese on my property. To my amazement, there was the goose with the broken and twisted leg along with a group of newfound friends. The goose seemed perfectly content. The bird stood tall and seemed to reflect an attitude of pride. It had adjusted to its handicap. It did not give up!

Matthew 6:25-26 I say to you, do not be worried about your life, as to what you will eat or what you will drink; nor for your body, as to what you will put on. Is not life more than food, and the body more than clothing? [26] Look at the birds of the air, that they do not sew, nor reap, nor gather into barns, and yet your Heavenly Father feeds them. Are you not worth much more than they?

Do you ever feel like the wounded goose? Do you feel handicapped? Handicaps come in many forms. Are you handicapped with a broken heart?

Your Heavenly Father is there for you. He knows your handicap. He knows your broken heart.

Trust God and stand tall like the wounded goose.

Matthew 6:34 Do not worry about tomorrow; for tomorrow will care for itself. Each day has enough trouble of its own.

Words of Life

People are gifted in various ways.

Some are gifted with an unusual ability to communicate succinctly with words.

But expression through words, spoken or written, are not the best form of communication.

The greatest impact you can ever have are the words of your life.

The Image of God

As we walk the path of life, we may traverse mountains and plains or encounter vast oceans to cross. But before we occupy one inch of space, before we inherit one minute of time that was chosen beforehand by the creator, we are designed in his image.

We may be tall or short, large or small, black or white, but we are all created by Love Himself. Each person is uniquely crafted by the Potter. But every soul designed and created has the ability to choose the love of life or mere existence. God chose to create us just as we are. But we all have the choice to relish life as we travel down whatever path we take.

I would rather live one day in the image of God's unexplainable love than merely exist forever.

www.ingramcontent.com/pod-product-compliance
Lightning Source LLC
Chambersburg PA
CBHW050034090426
42735CB00022B/3484